A gentleman may feel the need for a snack at a moment's notice ...

TIPPLES & TREATS
for the
English Gentleman

Copper Beech Publishing

Published in Great Britain by
Copper Beech Publishing Ltd
© Copper Beech Publishing Ltd 1999

Compiled by Sarah Fielding

All rights reserved
Without limiting the rights reserved under copyright above,
no part of this publication may be reproduced, stored in
or introduced into a retrieval system or transmitted
in any form or by any means without the prior written
consent of the publisher.

ISBN 1 898617 24-4

A CIP catalogue record for this book is available from the
British Library.

Copper Beech Publishing Ltd
P O Box 159 East Grinstead
Sussex England RH19 4FS

CONTAINING

Breakfast time
~ a gentleman's breakfast in
Spring, Summer, Autumn, Winter
~ a sportsman's breakfast
~ yachtsman's early morning punch

Luncheon
~ beverages at luncheon
~ when a bachelor entertains
~ oysters

Dinner & supper
~ the secrets of success
~ wines for dinner
~ stimulating the appetite
~ other delicacies
~ cheese
~ fruits
~ coffee & liqueurs

Social drinks
~ claret cups
~ traditional drinks
~ punch
~ champagne cups
a gentleman's remedies

BREAKFAST TIME

At breakfast ...

Breakfast is always a pleasant meal, both in winter and summer, spring and autumn; each season brings its particular enjoyment.

A refined gentlemen will always appreciate the delightful mixture of the lively and the snug in coming into the breakfast-room of a cold morning.

One of the first requisites for enjoyment at that period of the day and season, is a good fire and seeing everything prepared: a blazing grate, a clean table cloth and tea-things, together with tempting foods spread thereon.

Even if alone ...

Even if alone, it is certainly a delicious thing for a gentleman to resume an entertaining book at a particularly interesting passage, with a hot cup of tea at his elbow, and a piece of buttered toast in his hand. The first look at the page, accompanied by a co-existent bite of the toast, comes under the head of intensities!

for the English Gentleman

A GENTLEMAN'S BREAKFAST IN SPRING

Broiled trout
Codfish cakes
Curried eggs
Potted char
Potted beef
Stewed kidneys
Pommes de terre frites
Savoury omelette
Ox-palates
Marmalade
Water-cresses
Pigeon pie
Ham
Spiced beef

Tipples & Treats

A breakfast-room should, if possible, be so situated as to catch the early rays of the sun.

for the English Gentleman

The special treat of the early morning sun ...

In summer the morning can be a specially calm time; imagine being able to enter a sunny, cheerful room with its wide-open window, through which enters the cool, fresh morning air.

Add to this the scent of flowers and the song of the birds; the table prettily decked with buds and blossoms; luscious, tempting fruit lying *perdu* in a nest of green leaves; crisp rolls and golden butter, together with the more substantial dishes; all of which should look quite able to stand the vigorous attack of any gentleman!

*No one was conceited
before one o'clock in the day.*
Sydney Smith

Tipples & Treats

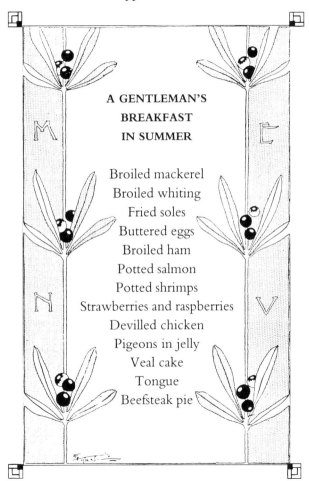

A GENTLEMAN'S BREAKFAST IN SUMMER

Broiled mackerel
Broiled whiting
Fried soles
Buttered eggs
Broiled ham
Potted salmon
Potted shrimps
Strawberries and raspberries
Devilled chicken
Pigeons in jelly
Veal cake
Tongue
Beefsteak pie

for the English Gentleman

Freshness and vigour ...

How cosy and enjoyable all this is! Added to these external sources of pleasure there is that most powerful spring of happiness of all, the innate sense of freshness and vigour which most gentlemen feel at that hour of the day, when a night's rest has refreshed tired bodies and soothed weary minds.

Yes, whether a gentleman joins the gathering round the table one of many, or sits down to it a solitary bachelor, the breakfast hour is a pleasant one.

The Ordinary Breakfast ...

At an ordinary breakfast the gentlemen help themselves and the ladies also. The various eatables such as eggs, potted meats and fish are placed up and down the table. These are interspersed with racks of dry toast, hot rolls, teacakes and muffins, and brown and white bread, with dainty pats of butter within easy reach.

The hot dishes (kidneys, mushrooms, fried bacon) are placed upon the table. The more substantial dishes, such as hams and pies, are placed on a white cloth on the sideboard.

Before each person is set a china plate, on which is placed a knife and fork with a table-napkin beside it. The plates for the meats are placed in small piles on the sideboard, so that at breakfast two plates are used at the same time.

for the English Gentleman

**A GENTLEMAN'S
BREAKFAST
IN AUTUMN**

Broiled fresh herrings
Collared eels
Poached eggs
Potted hare
Potted lobster
Toasted mushrooms
Broiled pheasant
Reindeer tongue
Fresh shrimps
Grapes
Grouse pie
Cold roast fowl
Ham
Rolled beef

Tipples & Treats

In France ...

The *petit déjeuner* is invariably commenced with an egg. A boiled egg is placed before everybody, and *everybody* eats a boiled egg. Then the vegetables are handed - asparagus - delicious sauce as an accompaniment, or pommes de terre frites. After this hot fish, then meats, lastly, fruits.

The cups and saucers are placed beside each person, and not in formal array in front of the lady presiding, and the teapot is passed round, together with the sugar and cream.

There is one thing to be learned with advantage from the French mode of serving breakfast, and that is the liberal supply of plates. They are worthy of imitation in this particular respect by those who are inclined to be stingy with the supply of clean plates!

for the English Gentleman

If one thing has touched an *assiette*, another must not be placed upon it!

Tipples & Treats

*'Plenty to look at,
plenty to eat
and plenty to leave.'*

Lancashire Breakfast Motto

A Sportsman's Breakfast …

The sportsman requires a substantial start in preparation for a long day away from the house.

In this instance, the table is never decorated or ornamented; all the space is reserved for the dishes, which on these occasions should make the table groan!

No sweets are placed on the table, only substantial food. Game pie is a standard dish, cold beef, devilled turkey, broiled ham, French pies, &c.

Cherry brandy is at hand for those who choose that as their beverage, and tankards of beer; but sportsmen now-a-days often take tea and coffee.

Tipples & Treats

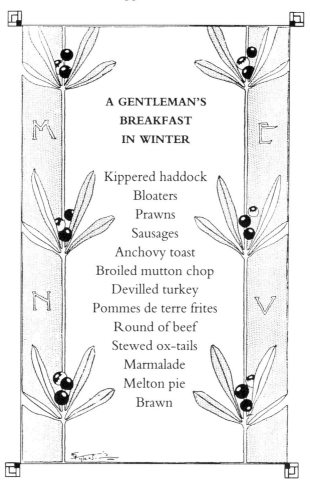

A GENTLEMAN'S BREAKFAST IN WINTER

Kippered haddock
Bloaters
Prawns
Sausages
Anchovy toast
Broiled mutton chop
Devilled turkey
Pommes de terre frites
Round of beef
Stewed ox-tails
Marmalade
Melton pie
Brawn

for the English Gentleman

A BREAKFAST TIME RECIPE (1875)

Anchovy Toast with Eggs
6 Eggs
1 cup butter drawn in milk
Rounds of stale bread
 (toasted and buttered)
Anchovy paste
Pepper and salt

Spread the buttered toast with the anchovy paste and with this cover the bottom of a flat dish. Heat the butter in a bain-marie.

Stir in eggs beaten very light.

Season to taste and heat, stirring all the time until they form a thick sauce. Do not let them boil. Pour over the toast and send to table very hot.

A favourite breakfast with most gentlemen!

A RECIPE FOR PUNCH AT BREAKFAST

Yachtsman's Early Morning Punch
2 glasses sherry
Yolks 2 eggs
Teaspoon powdered sugar
Grated nutmeg
Small knobs of ice

Shake well in a jug till mixed.

for the English Gentleman

At the luncheon table,
an elegant disorder is perfectly distinct
from a vulgar confusion.

for the English Gentleman

LUNCHEON

Gentlemen continue their conversation ...

Most gentlemen appreciate an absence of formality about an ordinary luncheon. The gentlemen do not take in the ladies but are able to enter the luncheon room in a body together and therefore continue their conversation.

If a hot luncheon is required, soup may be brought to table together with fish cakes, hashed mutton, minced chicken, mutton chops, or any entrée and light puddings.

Cold meats and sweets are oftentimes preferred.

Tipples & Treats

Any of the following may be selected for the luncheon table: cold lamb, pigeon, pork, beefsteak pies; pressed or roasted beef, tongue, fowls (boiled or roasted), game, potted meats, lobsters, salad, fruit tarts, puddings, custard, stewed fruit jelly, blancmange, cheesecakes, plum cake, cheese, biscuits, butter and fruits.

Beverages at luncheon ...

The beverages offered should be sherry, claret, claret cup and light beer.

When a bachelor entertains ...

The well-off man may wish to order cold delicacies and even a luncheon hamper from one of the well-known establishments. They can even be supplied with tablecloths, knives, forks, plates, napkins &c. This can provide a delightful alfresco meal.

for the English Gentleman

A gentleman may feel the need for a snack at a moment's notice. The appropriate servant should ensure that the larder is stocked with plenty of tempting foods.

OYSTERS

The oyster is a much favoured delicacy and can be eaten the moment it is opened (if it is to be eaten raw), with its own liquor in the undershell.

Or, if preferred, oysters may be served to be eaten with a small dinner-fork. The shell should be steadied on the plate with the fingers of the left hand and the oysters eaten whole. Lemon, cayenne pepper and bread are generally handed with oysters.

MUCH USED RECIPE FOR OYSTER AND EEL PIE

Make puff paste and lay it in your dish. Take great eels, clean them, cut in pieces and wash dry. Lay some butter in your pie and season the eels with some pepper, salt, nutmeg, cloves and mace. Cover it all over with great oysters and add more of the beaten spices and salt. Cover the whole with butter and put in two to three spoonfuls of white wine. Close it with paste, bake and serve it hot.

Tipples & Treats

RECIPE FOR OYSTER SOUP (1890)

Take 50 oysters, blanch them but do not let them boil, strain through a sieve and keep some of the liquor.

Put a quarter pound of butter into a stewpan; when it is melted, add 6oz flour and stir it over the fire for a few minutes; add the liquor from the oysters, 2 quarts of stock, 1 quart of new milk; season with salt, peppercorns, a little cayenne pepper, a blade of mace and essence of anchovy.

Strain, and let it boil 10 minutes. Put the oysters into the tureen with a gill of cream, and pour the boiling soup upon them.

DINNER & SUPPER

The secrets of success ...

The globe has been ransacked 'from China to Peru' for delicacies, novelties and varieties of comestibles and beverages. Money can now command meats, vegetables and fruits at every season of the year, and every wine that can gladden the heart of man.

But sumptuous foods and rare wines alone will not ensure an enjoyable dinner; and, indeed their importance is greatly over-estimated by the majority of dinner-givers.

A true gentleman will know that the guests feel no better nor enjoy their entertainment any the more for eating gold!

for the English Gentleman

Asparagus at a shilling a stalk, peaches ten shillings a piece and strawberries at two guineas a basket may be things to be boasted of by the purchaser but they may not be appreciated as real luxuries if they are unnaturally forced.

Good company, good waiting and good cookery are the true secrets of success!

Wines for dinner ...

Bad cookery is deleterious, but bad wines are positively poisonous! A well informed gentleman will have obtained good wines from a merchant of undoubted respectability.

No wine is placed on the dinner table, and it is the province of the butler to hand it, the proper kind at the proper time.

Both decanters and glasses must be kept faultlessly clean and the choice of wine is, of course, an individual one and the following is only a general guide.

for the English Gentleman

Champagne should be produced at
the very beginning of dinner.

With SOUPS ~ Sherry can be offered.

With OYSTERS ~ Serve Champagne.
With FISH ~ Light wines such as Hock,
Chablis and Sauterne.

With a PORK ROAST ~ Champagne should
be served.
With BEEF, LAMB OR GAME ~ A good Claret.

With DESSERT ~ Port wine *never* makes
its appearance until dessert, when sherry,
madeira and claret may also be served.

Claret cup is offered at intervals until
the conclusion of dinner.

Stimulating the appetite ...

Hors-d'oeuvres can be especially popular with the gentlemen. They should appear before anything else, to stimulate the appetite.

A few oysters can be sent round if they are in season, otherwise, their place is taken by other appetising temptations such as prawns, anchovies, sardines or olives.

Other delicacies ...

A gentleman may wish to consider serving asparagus - or artichokes (although these can be difficult vegetables to eat nicely!)

Cheese ...

When cheese is served, only the very best will do; guests may help themselves and can push deliciously small pieces with the knife-end on to small pieces of bread or biscuit.

Fruits ...

Fruits are always a delight and will make a tempting display.

Grapes in their own green leaves, strawberries piled high on their respective dishes, peaches, apricots and plums ensconced each in a separate leaf, so that they may not be robbed of their delicate bloom by too close contact with their fellows.

After dinner delicacies ...

On the table from the beginning of dinner should be the after dinner delicacies:

Crystallised fruits sparkling their best in showy boxes, walnuts and filberts with no decoration and a bowl of crystallised violets will always be appreciated.

Sherry ...

Sherry is improved by being decanted not less than two hours before it is required for use.

Cigars ...

Well-to-do hosts offer cigars and only the best brands should be provided.

for the English Gentleman

Coffee and Liqueurs ...

When coffee is served, the gentleman expects to have the cups heated in advance.

When the gentleman indicates he is ready, the servants should have ready the tray of coffee cups and each guest helps himself to sugar, milk and cream.

The head-servant follows with a smaller tray on which is the coffee and the guest once again helps himself. A third servant follows with the liqueurs.

RECIPE FOR
A FISHERMAN'S DINNER

Grilled Salmon Steak and Sauce

Procure the salmon you wish to use, remembering that the quantity in this recipe is for a pound, or a little over.

Wipe the salmon with a clean cloth and pour over it a gill of oil on a plate. Turn the fish so that both sides are oiled, then season with pepper and salt. Next see that you heat the gridiron on both sides, so that the fish will not stick in cooking. Place the fish on the gridiron and let it grill for twenty minutes, turning from time to time.

Before serving remove the bone from the centre, set it on a platter and garnish with parsley and pieces of cucumber.

RECIPE FOR
A FISHERMAN'S DINNER

The sauce

Take two yolks of eggs in a basin, work slightly with a wooden spoon and season with salt, pepper and made mustard. Work in gradually a dessertspoonful of best vinegar, and a gill of salad oil, drop by drop.

When the sauce is a thick cream and all the oil is used, stir in a dessertspoonful of tarragon vinegar. Chop together capers, gherkins and a little chilli, till you have rather over a tablespoonful, add to the sauce and place all in a tureen.

Tipples & Treats

SOCIAL DRINKS ~ CLARET CUPS

Mulled Claret is an excellent thing and most suitable to the Christmas Season.

Mulled Claret

Into a stewpan put 3 bruised cloves, half a stick of cinnamon, the peel of a lemon, 4 oz loaf sugar and ½ pint water. Boil for a quarter of an hour then add a little grated nutmeg, a pint of Claret and a wine glass of port wine. When nearly boiled, strain on toasted bread.

Hot Claret Cup

Mix together 2 bottles of Claret, 6 drops essence of ginger, ½ gill ginger syrup and a quart of boiling water

Tipples & Treats

Claret Cup for a party of twenty

Put into a large vessel imbedded in a mixture of ice and salt - the proportion of 3lb of salt to 12lb of ice is a very good one - some sprigs of balm and borage, or slices of cucumber (not too much, or it will render the drink disagreeably over-herbed); pour on the herbs 1 pint of sherry, ½ pint of brandy; then the peel of a lemon rubbed off lightly, with a lump of sugar (oleo-saccharum)★ add the strained juice of 1 lemon and 3 oranges, ½ pint of Curacao, 1 gill of ratafia of raspberries, 2 bottles of German seltzer water, 3 bottles of soda, and 3 bottles of claret; sweeten to taste; draw the 'herbing' and serve. *This can be made with champagne, use noyeau instead of ratafia of raspberries.*

★ Oleo-saccharum is the sugared essence of lemon and orange peel made by rubbing a piece of sugar on the outer rind of the fruit, and scraping as it absorbs the essential oil.

Claret Cup ...

Bruise 1 dozen cloves, ½ dozen allspice, add to 1 gill of sherry, and ½ gill of pale brandy; in three hours strain and prepare the oleo-saccharum of 2 lemons.

Into a vessel (imbedded in ice) put a few young borage leaves and a sprig of verbena (aloysia citridora) pour on the spirit and a liqueur-glassful of noyeau, Curacao, or Maraschino, add ¼lb pounded sugar, the oleo-saccharum and juice (strained) of 3 lemons, 3 bottles of claret, sweeten to taste; withdraw the herbing, add 1 bottle of champagne, 2 bottles of soda-water, 1½ pint lumps of ice, cover close, serve as soon as possible.

Cambridge Claret Cup

1 bottle of claret, ½ bottle of sherry, one gill of port, one gill of cherry-brandy, oleosaccharum and strained juice of one lemon; sweeten to taste; add cucumber and verbena sufficient to flavour; strain, ice up. When ready for use, add 3 bottles of iced German seltzer water.

Oxford Claret Cup

2 bottles of claret, pint of dry sherry, ½ gill of brandy, 1 bottle of champagne (iced) ½ gill of noyeau; infuse some young borage and balm leaves in the sherry; when sufficiently herbed, strain; add this to the claret, sweeten to taste, add the noyeau and spirit, ice up.

Just before serving, add 2 bottles of iced potash water, 1 pint of shaven ice and the champagne. Serve immediately.

for the English Gentleman

SOCIAL DRINKS ~ TRADITIONAL

The Cricketers' Cup

Mix together 1 bottle or quart of ale, 2 glasses sherry, 1 spoon cloves, 2 bottles ginger beer. Add a small quantity of grated nutmeg on top and some pieces of pure spring block ice before serving.

Egg-nogg

Hot Egg-nogg (Auld Man's Milk): heat 1 pint of Scotch ale; add while warming ¼oz bruised cinnamon, ¼oz grated nutmeg, ¼oz powdered ginger; beat up the yolks of 2 eggs with a little brown sugar; pour in the ale gradually; when well mixed, add 1 glass of whisky.

Iced Egg-nogg

Beat up the yolk of 1 egg with a tablespoonful of cold water and the same of pounded white sugar; add 1 gill of sherry or ½ gill of brandy, same of rum, ¼ pint good milk. Mix together, add ¼ pint shaven (or pulverised) ice.

Bottled Velvet

Bottled Velvet is made of one bottle of Moselle, ½ pint of dry sherry, thin peel of 1 lemon, 2 tablespoonfuls of sugar; mix when sufficiently flavoured, and strain; add ice, and serve up.

Cider Nectar

Take 1 quart cider, 1 bottle soda-water, 1 glass of sherry, 1 small glass of brandy, juice of ½ a lemon (strained), ¼ of a lemon rubbed on sugar, sugar and nutmeg to taste; a sprig of verbena; flavour it to taste with extract of pine-apple; strain and ice well.

A drink to delight guests!

Porter

Good porter needs no praise and bottled porter, iced, is in hot weather most refreshing.

Whene'er a bowl of punch we make,
Four striking opposites we take -
The strong, the small, the sharp,
the sweet,
Together mixed, most kindly meet.
And when they happily unite,
The bowl is 'fragrant with delight'.

SOCIAL DRINKS ~ PUNCH

A delicious beverage ...

A gentleman will wish to offer his guests a glass of punch as they arrive for a party. This delicious beverage is a composition of sugar, lemon, water or milk and spirit, with the addition of some aromatic or cordial; wine being sometimes substituted for the spirit.

Punch à la Regent (1820)

Take 4oz of clarified sugar, thin peel of 1 lemon and 1 Seville orange, 1 bottle of dry champagne, ½ bottle of white brandy, ½ gill of rum, ½ gill of arrack, ½ gill of pineapple syrup, 1 wine glass of Maraschino; pour 1 quart of boiling water over 2 teaspoonfuls of green tea; let it stand five minutes, strain, and mix with other ingredients. Pass through a sieve, let it remain in ice 30 minutes.

Royal Punch

1½ pints of green tea, ½ pint of brandy, ¼ pint pineapple rum, ¼ pint Curacao, ¼ pint arrack, juice of 2 lemons (strained), the peel of 1 rubbed off on sugar. Warm, and add 1 gill of calves foot jelly; serve hot.

Regent's Punch

1 bottle of sparkling champagne, 1 bottle of hock, 1 gill of dry sherry, 1 gill of pale brandy, ½ gill of rum, 1 gill of lemon juice, ½ gill of Curacao, quart of green tea, 1 bottle of seltzer water, sugar to taste; ice to the utmost!

Vanilla Punch

Infuse a stick of vanilla in ½ pint of pale brandy; when sufficiently flavoured, strain; add a sherbet of lemon juice and sugar. Fill a tumbler with shaven ice and use straws!

Apple Punch

Into a jug, lay slices of apples and lemons alternately. Strew between each layer some powdered sugar-candy; pour over them a bottle of either Claret, Chablis or Roussillon and ½ gill of brandy. After four hours, strain with pressure.

Orange Punch

Strain the juice of 6 oranges; rub sufficiently off the rind of a Seville or Mandarin orange to impart a pleasing flavour; add 1 drop of essence of neroli, 1 pint of brandy, 1 pint of orange shrub; sweeten to taste, and add as much liquor as desired.

Punch, if compounded in a
proper manner,
is not so intoxicating as it has
the character of being.

SOCIAL DRINKS ~ CHAMPAGNE CUPS

Champagne Cup

Take one bottle sparkling champagne, (iced), one bottle of soda water (iced) 2 oz powdered sugar, sprig of borage and balm, juice and thin peel of one lemon; pour the champagne on the lemon, sugar and herbs; cover the vessel, (which is in ice) till the sugar is dissolved. Add the soda water.

Champagne Cup 2

2 bottles of sparkling champagne (iced), ½ pint of strawberry or lemon water ice, 2 bottles soda water. Mix well and use immediately.

A GENTLEMAN'S REMEDIES

A treat to cheer the spirits ...

Borage is a plant of coarse appearance and bears a pretty blue flower. It is found growing wild and by people keeping bees. It is said to possess medicinal properties and to be very cheering to the spirits! A few sprigs of borage in bloom infuse a cooling taste in wine cups.

To fortify ...

To strengthen the system which has 'fallen below par' - take oysters and champagne!

A gentleman's remedy for colds ...

Ale Posset is made with ½ pint of dry sherry, ½ pint clear ale and a quart of boiled cream mixed with spices. Strain through a tammy.

for the English Gentleman

A GENTLEMAN'S REMEDIES

To assuage pain in the head ...
Sugared violets will assuage the pains of the head and other inward parts.

TIPPLES & TREATS ...

The Loving Cup ...

The Loving Cup is a splendid feature of the Hall feasts of the City and Inns of Court. The cup is of silver and is filled with spiced wine, immemorially termed 'sack'. Immediately the Master and Wardens drink to their visitors a hearty welcome; the cup is then passed round the table, and each guest, after he has drunk, applies his table-napkin to the mouth of the cup before he passes it to his neighbour.

Oysters as a gift ...

Romans were in the habit of sending presents of oysters to their friends, who, it is probable, returned the compliment in the shape of a boar's head, fat ducks or other welcome produce of the farm.

Wines ...

Next to water and milk, wine is certainly the most ancient beverage in the world. Of its actual discovery nothing is known. The earliest record of its use is that given in Genesis ix 20: 'Noah planted a vineyard and drank of the vine.'

Beer ...

Beer is often spoken of as the National Beverage of England, and is the common drink of a vast number. There is probably no other article of consumption about which so many fallacies are current as about beer. Sometimes it has been deemed a food equal, if not superior, to bread. Thousands are under the impression that it gives them muscular strength and mental ability. Tens of thousands use it for the simple reason that they 'like it' and undoubtedly the love is beer is ingrained in the nation, the result of centuries of use.

Whistle for it ...

'If you want any more you must whistle for it' came from a vessel having a whistle attached to it, which was blown when it required replenishing: it was called the 'whistle tankard'.

Taking wine ...

The practice of taking wine together was prevalent amongst the Greeks and the Anglo-Saxons and the latter always accompanied the ceremony with a kiss. A writer of King Henry VIII's day in laying down the rules of etiquette, suggests as one of them, that when any one will drink to the health of another he must fix his eye upon him for a moment and give him time, if it be possible, to swallow his morsel!

for the English Gentleman

THE ETIQUETTE COLLECTION
All these and more ... collect the set!

ETIQUETTE FOR COFFEE LOVERS
Fresh coffee - the best welcome in the world!
Enjoy the story of coffee drinking,
coffee etiquette and recipes.

ETIQUETTE FOR CHOCOLATE LOVERS
Temptation through the years.
A special treat for all Chocolate Lovers.

THE ETIQUETTE OF NAMING THE BABY
'A good name keeps its lustre in the dark.'
Old English Proverb

THE ETIQUETTE OF AN ENGLISH TEA
How to serve a perfect English afternoon tea;
traditions, superstitions, recipes and how to read your
fortune in the tea-leaves afterwards.

THE ETIQUETTE OF ENGLISH PUDDINGS
Traditional recipes for good old-fashioned
puddings - together with etiquette notes for serving.

ETIQUETTE FOR GENTLEMEN
*'If you have occasion to use your handkerchief
do so as noiselessly as possible.'*

FINE BRITISH GIFT BOOKS

HOW TO ENTERTAIN YOUR GUESTS
Edwardian parlour games

THE DUTIES OF SERVANTS
An authentic Victorian guide containing the many rules for an efficient and well-run household!

MANGLES MOPS & FEATHER BRUSHES
Household hints
- for the housework and the laundry.
Use everyday items from the kitchen storecupboard to clean your home!

THE GENTLE ART OF FLIRTATION
Flirts today will enjoy this collection of advice and sayings from days gone by.

RECIPES FOR GARDENERS
Trusted hints and recipes - perfect for any keen gardener.

For your free catalogue, write to

Copper Beech Publishing Ltd
P O Box 159 East Grinstead Sussex England RH19 4FS

*Copper Beech Gift Books
are designed and printed
in Great Britain.*